A Life Well Lived
Bible Companion

Discover the Rewards of an Obedient Heart

BASED ON THE BOOK BY

CHARLES R. SWINDOLL

Produced in association with CREA~
Insight for Livin

THOMAS NELSON
Since 1798

NASHVILLE   DALLAS   MEXICO CITY   RIO DE JANEIRO   BEIJING

A Life Well Lived
Discover the Rewards of an Obedient Heart
Bible Companion

© 2007 by Charles R. Swindoll, Inc.

Published in Nashville, Tennessee, by Thomas Nelson. Thomas Nelson is a trademark of Thomas Nelson, Inc.

Thomas Nelson, Inc., titles may be purchased in bulk for educational, business, fund-raising, or sales promotional use. For information, please e-mail SpecialMarkets@ThomasNelson.com.

Published in association with Yates & Yates, LLP, Attorneys and Counselors, Orange, California.

A Life Well Lived Bible Companion

ISBN 978-1-4185-3099-0

Printed in the United States of America

07 08 09 10 11 RRD 5 4 3 2 1

From the Bible-Teaching Ministry of Charles R. Swindoll

Charles R. Swindoll has devoted his life to the clear, practical teaching and application of God's Word and His grace. A pastor at heart, Chuck has served as senior pastor to congregations in Texas, Massachusetts, and California. He currently pastors Stonebriar Community Church in Frisco, Texas, but Chuck's listening audience extends far beyond a local church body. As a leading program in Christian broadcasting, *Insight for Living* airs in major Christian radio markets around the world, reaching people groups in languages they can understand. Chuck's extensive writing ministry has also served the body of Christ worldwide and his leadership as president and now chancellor of Dallas Theological Seminary has helped prepare and equip a new generation for ministry. Chuck and Cynthia, his partner in life and ministry, have four grown children and ten grandchildren.

Based on the original outlines, charts, and transcripts of Charles R. Swindoll's sermons, the Bible Companion text was developed and written by Michael J. Svigel, Th.M., Ph.D., Dallas Theological Seminary.

Editor in Chief: Cynthia Swindoll, President, Insight for Living
Executive Vice President: Wayne Stiles, Th.M., D.Min., Dallas Theological Seminary
Theological Editor: John Adair, Th.M., Ph.D. candidate, Dallas Theological Seminary
Content Editor: Brie Engeler, M.A., Biblical Studies, Dallas Theological Seminary
Project Supervisor, Creative Ministries: Cari Harris, B.A., Journalism, Grand Canyon University

OTHER BOOKS BY THE AUTHOR

Books for Adults

Active Spirituality

Bedside Blessings

Behold . . . The Man!

The Bride

Come Before Winter

Compassion: Showing We Care in a
Careless World

The Darkness and the Dawn

David: A Man of Passion and Destiny

Day by Day

Dear Graduate

Dropping Your Guard

Elijah: A Man of Heroism and Humility

Encourage Me

Encouragement for Life

Esther: A Woman of Strength and Dignity

Fascinating Stories of Forgotten Lives

The Finishing Touch

Five Meaningful Minutes a Day

Flying Closer to the Flame

For Those Who Hurt

Getting Through the Tough Stuff

God's Provision

The Grace Awakening

The Grace Awakening Devotional

Great Attitudes!

Great Days with Great Lives

Growing Deep in the Christian Life

Growing Strong in the Seasons of Life

Growing Wise in Family Life

Hand Me Another Brick

Hand Me Another Brick Bible Companion

Home: Where Life Makes Up Its Mind

Hope Again

Improving Your Serve

Intimacy with the Almighty

Job: A Man of Heroic Endurance

Joseph: A Man of Integrity and Forgiveness

Killing Giants, Pulling Thorns

Laugh Again

Leadership: Influence That Inspires

Living Above the Level of Mediocrity

Living Beyond the Daily Grind, Books I
and II

The Living Insights Study Bible, general editor

Living on the Ragged Edge

Living on the Ragged Edge
Workbook

Make Up Your Mind

Man to Man

Marriage: From Surviving to Thriving

Marriage: From Surviving to Thriving
Workbook

Moses: A Man of Selfless Dedication

The Mystery of God's Will

Parenting: From Surviving to Thriving

Parenting: From Surviving to Thriving
Workbook

Paul: A Man of Grace and Grit

The Quest for Character

Recovery: When Healing Takes Time

The Road to Armageddon
Sanctity of Life
Shedding Light on Our Dark Side
Simple Faith
Simple Trust
So, You Want to Be Like Christ?
Starting Over
Start Where You Are
The Strength of Character:
  7 Essential Traits of a Remarkable Life
Strengthening Your Grip
Stress Fractures
Strike the Original Match
The Strong Family
Suddenly One Morning
Swindoll's Ultimate Book of Illustrations
  and Quotes
Three Steps Forward, Two Steps Back
Victory: A Winning Game Plan for Life
Why, God?
Wisdom for the Way
You and Your Child

Mini Books

Abraham: A Model of Pioneer Faith
David: A Model of Pioneer Courage
Esther: A Model of Pioneer Independence
Moses: A Model of Pioneer Vision
Nehemiah: A Model of Pioneer
  Determination

Booklets

Anger
Attitudes
Commitment
Dealing with Defiance
Demonism
Destiny
Divorce
Eternal Security
Forgiving and Forgetting
Fun Is Contagious!
God's Will
Hope
Impossibilities
Integrity
Leisure
The Lonely Whine of the Top Dog
Make Your Dream Come True
Making the Weak Family Strong
Moral Purity
Peace . . . in Spite of Panic
Portrait of a Faithful Father
The Power of a Promise
Prayer
Reflections from the Heart:
  A Prayer Journal
Seeking the Shepherd's Heart:
  A Prayer Journal
Sensuality
Stress
This Is No Time for Wimps
Tongues
When Your Comfort Zone Gets the Squeeze
Woman

Contents

A Letter from Chuck

What does a well lived life look like?

Depending on who you ask, you'll receive scores of answers. Today, people everywhere are sharing their ideas about what makes life worth living. Religions and world-views collide in a storm of competing thoughts. Anyone with Internet access can blog about his or her beliefs. The intensity of competing voices is reaching a feverish pitch.

But hold on! *What about God's voice?* What does our Creator expect of us? How can we live well according to His perspective?

Today in a world that's lost its way, God's perspective on life easily becomes marginalized. Biblical virtues of courage, kindness, humility, and integrity are shoved aside in favor of political correctness, personal choice, individual pride, financial accomplishment, and simply "feeling good."

In a cultural climate similar to our own, the Old Testament prophet Micah confronted God's people, offering a prescription for living life well in the midst of a crooked generation. God's voice speaks just as loudly to New Testament believers today as it did to the Old Testament saints long ago:

What does the LORD require of you
But to do justice, to love kindness,
And to walk humbly with your God?
(Micah 6:8)

As you open this Bible companion and dig deeply into the principles of God's Word, take time to learn the real characteristics of an authentic life from heroes like Peter, Joseph, David, and Daniel. When you discover what God expects of you, my hope is that you'll not only know what a life well lived looks like . . . but you'll be able to *experience* it as well.

CHARLES R. SWINDOLL

How to Use This Bible Companion

Doing what's right . . . showing mercy . . . living humbly . . . modeling integrity. These qualities of a well lived life don't come naturally or quickly. Cultivating the character qualities that mature us into the kind of people God expects us to be requires close attention to moment-by-moment decisions. We have to constantly focus our minds, hearts, and wills on solid biblical principles in order to get us from where we are today to where we ought to be. In four focused lessons, this Bible companion will help you along the path of spiritual maturity.

Whether you choose to complete these lessons individually or as part of a group, a brief introduction to the overall structure of each lesson will help you get the most out of these lessons.

LESSON ORGANIZATION

 The Heart of the Matter highlights the main idea of each lesson for rapid orientation. The lesson itself is then composed of two main teaching sections of insight and application.

Discovering the Way explores the principles of Scripture through observation and interpretation of the Bible passages and drawing out practical principles for life. Parallel passages and additional questions supplement the main Scriptures for a more in-depth study.

Starting Your Journey focuses on application to help you put into practice the principles of the lesson in ways that fit your personality, gifts, and level of spiritual maturity.

USING THE BIBLE COMPANION

A *Life Well Lived Bible Companion* is designed with individual study in mind, but it may also be adapted for group study. If you choose to use this Bible companion in a group setting, please keep in mind that many of the lessons ask personal, probing questions, seeking to elicit answers that reveal an individual's true character and challenge the reader to change. Care, therefore, should be taken by the group leader to prepare the group for the sensitive nature of these studies, to forgo certain questions if they appear to be too personal, and to remain perceptive to the mood and dynamics of the group if questions or answers become uncomfortable.

Whether you use this Bible Companion in groups or individually, we recommend the following method:

Prayer—Begin each lesson with prayer, asking God to teach you through His Word and to open your heart to the self-discovery afforded by the questions and text of the lesson.

Scripture—Have your Bible handy. We recommend the New American Standard Bible or another literal translation, rather than a paraphrase. As you progress through each lesson, the reading icon will prompt you to read relevant sections of Scripture and answer questions related to the topic. You also will want to look up Scripture passages noted in parentheses.

Questions—As you encounter the questions, approach them wisely and creatively. Not every question will be applicable to each person all the time. Use the questions as general guides in your thinking rather than rigid forms to complete. If there are things you just don't understand or that you want to explore further, be sure to jot down your thoughts or questions.

SPECIAL BIBLE COMPANION FEATURES

Throughout the chapters, you'll find several special features designed to add insight or depth to your study. These features will enhance your study and deepen your knowledge of Scripture, history, and theology.

DIGGING DEEPER

Various passages in Scripture touch on deeper theological questions or confront modern worldviews and philosophies that conflict with a biblical worldview. This feature will help you gain deeper insight into specific theological issues related to the biblical text.

DOORWAY TO HISTORY

Sometimes the chronological gap that separates us from the original author and readers clouds our understanding of a passage of Scripture. This feature takes you back in time to explore the surrounding history, culture, and customs of the biblical world.

Our prayer is that this Insight for Living *Bible Companion* will not only help you to dig deeper into God's Word but also provide insights and application for *real* life.

Lesson One

Doing What's Right

MICAH 6:8; ACTS 4:1–21

THE HEART OF THE MATTER

In Micah 6:8, the bold prophet answered a question many people wonder about today: What does the Lord expect of us? Micah's answer is comprehensive: God calls us to do justice, to love kindness, and to walk humbly with Him. The first of these three expectations requires us to do what is right, regardless of the consequences. We find an example of such courageous obedience illustrated for us in the lives of the first-century apostles.

DISCOVERING THE WAY

Today, idolatry of the most insidious kind is on the rise. Greed and avarice mark almost every action—even the "spiritual" ones. The pursuit of wealth drives people's lives—no principle is worth keeping, no rule worth respecting, if it stands in the way of profit. The world lacks integrity to such a degree that nobody can be trusted, not even those closest to you.

True believers are suffocated by religious charlatans preaching a watered-down message. Ungodliness and sin have become nouveau . . . and taking a stand for truth is passé. People don't want convicting, potentially offensive preaching, but weak, pandering words of affirmation. Popular preachers encourage the desire for wealth and prosperity and broker a "me-centered" morality. Bible teachers and those ordained to carry out the ministry of God are increasingly corrupt, selfish, immoral, and greedy—they fit in nicely with the culture around them. They are driven by money, comfort, popularity, and luxury.

The world appears to be falling apart.

Though these words could apply to our own twenty-first century world, they actually describe the eighth-century BC world of the prophet Micah. His lone voice—nearly lost among the blaring noise of sin around him—still speaks to us today as we seek to live life well, to please our God, and to do what He expects of us.

If you were to ask several Christians what God expects of us, what are some of the different answers you might expect to receive? Try to list at least five.

_____

_____

_____

_____

_____

_____

_____

_____

_____

Do you think these Christians would say that they personally are fulfilling God's expectations? Why, or why not?

_____

_____

_____

_____

_____

_____

_____

_____

MICAH: A MAJOR MINOR PROPHET

In Micah's day, God's people received warnings, instructions, and exhortations from the lips of prophets, whose messages were divinely inspired and infallible. In the New Testament period after Christ's resurrection and ascension, God gave messages to the church through apostles and prophets who had the same authority as the Old Testament prophets, speaking the very words of God. However, after the first century, the offices of prophet and apostle ceased, leaving us today with their prophetic writings in the Bible. Therefore, only the inspired Scriptures speak with absolute authority today.

Doorway to History
The Prophets and Their Message

Through the Old Testament prophets, believers are given a glimpse of God's overarching plan of history, constantly pointing forward to the Messiah and His coming kingdom of righteousness. The prophets also demonstrate how to live according to God's Word in tumultuous times. In many ways, their message is relevant to us today, as our world often mirrors the moral and spiritual conditions that they faced in their day.

As such, the prophets themselves are heroic examples for us as we live in this corrupt world. While politicians looked the other way and folded in the face of evil, prophets recognized wickedness and refused to compromise. While false priests went through the motions of religious legalism, prophets called the faithful to genuine devotion. While kings fed the flames of raging megalomania through self-serving corruption and cruelty, prophets pointed to the one object of adoration and worship: the Lord God.

Although Christians are not called to the office of prophet today, believers are called to have a prophetic voice for justice, kindness, and humility in a world that shouts defiantly against God's revelation.

Micah, a country preacher from the south, was called by God to champion the cause of the poor and oppressed. He shared their pain and refused to follow the example of the morally compromised political and religious leaders of the day. When we read Micah 6, we discover a "covenant lawsuit" in which the prophet, acting like a prosecuting attorney, summoned the people of Judah to hear the charge the Lord held against them. But rather than directly charging the nation with breaking the covenant, God first asked if they had any charge to bring against Him (Micah 6:1–3)!

While carrying on this figurative courtroom dialogue, Micah switched roles in verses 6 and 7, putting himself in the place of the people—acknowledging their obvious guilt and asking God several questions.

According to Micah 6:6–7, what did many people believe God expected of them?

_____

_____

_____

_____

_____

How is the attitude of some Christians regarding what God expects of us similar to that of the people in Micah's day? Think of specific examples you have observed and list them here.

_____

_____

_____

_____

_____

_____

THE LORD EXPECTS US
TO DO WHAT IS RIGHT

As we paint a picture of a life well lived, let's focus on the three things the Lord expected of His people in the tumultuous days of Micah and examine how those principles apply to us today.

Read Micah 6:8.

God expects His people to do justice, to love mercy, and to walk humbly before Him. Obviously, the Lord delights more in genuine attitudes of the heart that overflow into our relationships than in empty religious rituals or acts of sacrifice. Outward conduct is essential, of course, but its true worth always depends on inner character.

Read 1 Corinthians 13:1–3. What beliefs or actions did Paul declare to be useless without genuine love?

_____

_____

_____

_____

_____

_____

_____

_____

The first of God's expectations in Micah 6:8 is that we "do justice." The Hebrew word translated as "justice" is *mishpat*, which means "rightness rooted in God's character."[1] Thus, God's people were expected to do what is right, regardless of shifting cultural norms, the opinions of others, personal feelings, the availability of the path of least resistance, or even the sometimes arbitrary laws of a corrupt government. Rather, God's people were expected to act righteously based on the immovable teaching and character of God.

Where or in what does today's culture find its beliefs about right and wrong? Give a specific example from your personal life or from public figures.

_____
_____
_____
_____
_____
_____
_____
_____
_____

How would you respond to this view of right and wrong?

_____
_____
_____
_____
_____
_____
_____
_____
_____

Where do you think our understanding of right and wrong should come from?

_____

_____

_____

_____

_____

_____

_____

THE APOSTLES' EXAMPLE
OF DOING WHAT IS RIGHT

One of our greatest challenges as Christians living in a postmodern world, a world that shuns absolute truth, a world that doubts our ability to know right and wrong, is to become a people that do what is right . . . regardless of our circumstances or feelings. This can be extremely difficult. The apostles faced a similar cultural clash during the earliest days of the infant church.

When we raise the curtain on the dramatic events of Acts 4, Christ had already commissioned the apostles to preach the gospel throughout the world (Matthew 28:19–20; Acts 1:8). The Spirit had come and transformed the disciples into bold, public messengers for Christ, just as He had promised (Acts 2).

Read Acts 4:1–12.

The religious leaders in Jerusalem were alarmed at what the apostles were now preaching to the people. And understandably so, for they had instigated the trial and crucifixion of Jesus just over a month earlier.

Why do you think the priests, temple guard, and Sadducees were so disturbed by the apostles' preaching? (See Acts 4:2, 4, 7, 10 for clues.)

_____

_____

_____

_____

_____

_____

In what ways were the disciples doing "what was right"? How did they know they were on the right track?

_____

_____

_____

_____

_____

_____

_____

_____

_____

Read Acts 4:13–21.

The bold preaching of the apostles stupefied the religious leaders of Jerusalem. However, regardless of the apostles' eyewitness testimony, their appeals to the prophecies of Scripture, and their miraculous signs, those in authority commanded Peter and John to stop preaching about Jesus.

How did the disciples respond to the order to stop preaching? (See Acts 4:19–20.)

_____

_____

_____

_____

_____

_____

_____

_____

What do you think gave them the boldness to respond in this way?

_____

_____

_____

_____

_____

Digging Deeper
Should We Submit to Government?

God established human government, endowing it with the authority to punish wickedness, among other things. He did this, in part, to prevent the world from spiraling into the kind of chaos characterized by the days of Noah before the Flood (Genesis 6:5–6; Romans 13:3–4). Christians are instructed to submit to governing authorities at every level (Romans 13:1; 1 Peter 2:13). The purpose of this biblical instruction is not only for our own good (Romans 13:3), but also to silence those who unjustly persecute believers (1 Peter 2:15).

As we consider what the Bible says regarding a Christian's responsibility to submit to governing authority, we need to understand the full effect of this New Testament command on believers in the early church. Although they were being persecuted unjustly by the government, Christ instructed His followers to pay taxes, even to the pagan Roman Empire. And while the government continued to oppress the Jews and use their taxes to build temples and enforce the worship of Caesar (Matthew 22:21), believers in the decades following the apostles still held to the principle of submission to their governing authorities.

However, because of sin's presence in human government, believers often find themselves faced with the difficult choice either to obey God or man (Daniel 6; Acts 5:27–29). In cases where God has given His people a clear command in His Word, such as to share the gospel or to avoid idolatry, believers must obey God . . . and suffer the consequences of their civil disobedience.

As we move forward from the apostles toward our own twenty-first century context, let's stop along the way and take a brief look at one more hero of the faith who refused to back down when it came to clearly preaching the gospel of Jesus Christ: the German reformer, Martin Luther.

As a monk bound by the works-based religion he had inherited from the medieval Roman Catholic Church, Luther struggled to comprehend how a sinful man could stand under the scrutiny of a holy and exacting God. As a scholar, he began studying the Bible in the original languages and discovered several simple words that set him free: "But the righteous man shall live by faith" (Romans 1:17). Once he understood that righteousness is a gift that comes by faith in Christ alone—not by works—he heralded this message that we are justified by faith alone. And in response, he took a stand against the powerful Catholic Church for its unscriptural teachings that had abandoned the very words of the Bible!

At noon on October 31, 1517, Luther nailed his *Ninety-five Theses* to the door of Castle Church in Wittenberg, Germany, unaware of the profound influence it would have in the lives of Christians to this day. However, the Roman Catholic religious authorities were unimpressed with Luther's recovery of the true gospel. At the famous trial in the city of Worms, Luther was called upon to renounce his "heretical" theology: "Do you recant, or do you not?"

With the threat of imprisonment and execution hovering over his head, Luther announced:

Unless I am overcome by the testimonies of
Scripture or by clear reasoning—for I believe
neither the Pope nor the councils alone,
because it is clear as day that they have often
erred and contradicted themselves—I am overcome by the Holy Scriptures I have quoted. My
conscience is held captive by God's Word. I
cannot and will not recant anything, because it
is unsafe and dangerous to go against the conscience. Here I stand. I cannot do otherwise.
God help me! Amen.[2]

Luther's inspiring stand for the gospel against the threats
of religious and political rulers continues to inspire believers to take a stand for what they know to be right.

 STARTING YOUR JOURNEY
What can we remember and apply today about
doing what's right in a world bent on doing
what's wrong?

First, *it's necessary to know what is right.* The lines
between right and wrong have been blurred in our postmodern culture. We can't take cues from the world around
us to determine right and wrong. Instead, we must center
our thoughts, submit our wills, and conform our actions to

God's Word (2 Timothy 3:16). When we've done this, the Spirit will transform our minds, wills, and actions to conform to what is right. When the truth seeps into our hearts, we will naturally live it out. In addition, we need a close community of wise, godly friends to hold us accountable to God's Word (Hebrews 10:25). Their advice and counsel are invaluable as we travel the road of the Christian life together.

How would you respond to a Christian who says he or she discovers what's right by looking into his or her own heart? What part(s) of the means for knowing right and wrong is he or she missing?

Why is it dangerous to trust in your own feelings or "inner voice" for moral and personal direction?

_____

_____

_____

_____

_____

_____

_____

_____

_____

_____

Second, *it's wise to expect resistance.* Micah lived through rejection by his countrymen . . . the apostles faced beatings, imprisonment, and ultimately, execution . . . Luther endured trials and exile. In the same way, when you do what's right, you will face resistance. It may come in the form of subtle setbacks at the hands of agenda-driven rivals. Or it may come as severe personal attacks from those who despise Christianity. It can even come at the hand of religious elitists in the name of Christianity! Either way, we should never be surprised when resistance strikes.

Have you ever experienced resistance or paid a high price for choosing to do what was right? What happened? Did you take a stand? Why, or why not?

_____

_____

_____

_____

_____

_____

_____

_____

If you could go back and live through the situation again, would you do anything differently? If so, what would you change?

_____

_____

_____

_____

_____

_____

_____

Third, *it's reassuring to remember God is at work.* Even if it appears that the enemies of righteousness and justice are turning the world upside-down, we can be confident that God is still working to keep everything moving according to His plan. In fact, God can and will use any number of unexpected means for accomplishing His purpose. So when resistance comes, continue doing what's right in spite of your circumstances. God will ultimately work all things together for your good (Romans 8:28).

What are some present-day examples of moral, doctrinal, or social issues that require Christians to take a biblical stand and refuse to compromise with the world?

_____

_____

_____

_____

_____

_____

_____

_____

If one of these issues were to come up at a family gathering or at work, and people were arguing a non-biblical view, which one of the following quotes do you think would best characterize your typical response:

1. "Hmmmm . . ."

2. "Let's stop talking about these things!"

3. "You have a valid point. I think I'll reconsider my views."

4. "Well, I sort of think _____, but we're all entitled to our own opinions."

5. "I hear what you're saying, but here's what I believe about it and why."

6. "You're wrong! God said it, I believe it, that settles it!"

7. "Let's step outside and settle this the old-fashioned way . . ."

What is it about your experiences or personality that might influence your response?

_____

_____

_____

_____

_____

_____

_____

Will you commit today to not only discover what's right through accountability to God's Word and good counsel from God's people . . . but also to do what's right regardless of the cost? Write a statement describing your commitment here.

_____

_____

_____

_____

_____

_____

_____

_____

Doing what's right is rarely easy, and once a believer commits to taking a stand against the world's watered-down values of right and wrong, he or she can expect resistance. But in a corrupted world that has lost its way, Micah's exhortation and the example of the apostles should inspire us to do what's right in spite of the cost.

Lesson Two

Loving What's Kind

MICAH 6:8; GENESIS 49:28–50:21

THE HEART OF THE MATTER

Micah 6:8 reveals the second character quality God expects of us: kindness. Few things catch the attention or remain in the memory more readily than acts of kindness, but it sometimes seems that everything around us works to devalue or derail them. Of all the biblical examples that reflected amazing kindness, Joseph's relationship with his brothers may shine the brightest.

DISCOVERING THE WAY

An award-winning documentary follows the life story of a remarkable Holocaust survivor, Eva Mozes Kor. At the age of nine, Eva and her twin sister, Miriam, were plucked from the crowds at Auschwitz. Placed in the brutal hands of Dr. Joseph Mengele, they became human guinea pigs in his twisted "medical" experiments. Eva suffered the loss of her other family members, endured personal torture almost to the point of death, and stored up a haunting montage of painful memories. But at the liberation of Auschwitz, Eva and her sister emerged from the camp with other "Mengele Twins" scarred by fear, hatred, bitterness, and sadness—normal reactions to experiences of such extreme evil.

Fast-forward fifty years to a ceremony commemorating the liberation of Auschwitz. Eva did something that would

confuse, anger, and shock many of her fellow survivors—
she forgave Dr. Mengele.[1]

**Brainstorm seven to ten words that describe a bitter
person? What does he or she say or do that reveals his
or her inner attitude?**

_____

_____

_____

_____

_____

_____

_____

**Is there anybody from your past or present toward
whom you feel bitterness or unforgiveness? How do
these attitudes manifest themselves in your thoughts,
words, or actions? In your relationship with him or her?**

_____

_____

_____

_____

_____

_____

_____

Though very few have suffered to the extent of Auschwitz survivors, many of us have endured injustice, cruelty, or other acts of unkindness from those around us. Our natural response is to desire justice . . . or revenge. And when nothing happens, bitterness, resentment, anger, and sadness simmer deep inside our hearts. The one thing that can release these emotions and bring real healing is often the one thing we simply can't bring ourselves to do: *forgive*.

As we will see in this lesson, showing kindness, mercy, and forgiveness to those who least deserve it is just what God expects us to do.

GOD EXPECTS US TO LOVE KINDNESS

When Micah relayed to the people of Israel the three things the Lord expected from them, he said, "to do justice, to love kindness, and to walk humbly with your God" (Micah 6:8). The word *kindness* here is the Hebrew word *chesed*, which means "grace, goodness, or mercy."[2] Few things grab the attention of the world more quickly than unexpected acts of kindness. And people remember few things longer than being treated with extraordinary mercy. However, in spite of the powerful impact kindness has on others, it sometimes seems that everything in the world around us works overtime to prevent us from acting kindly.

What issues, circumstances, or emotions sometimes make it difficult for us to show kindness, mercy, and forgiveness to others?

_____

_____

_____

_____

_____

_____

_____

Kindness takes time, calls for compassion, focuses on others, and often includes forgiveness. God's Word is filled with many inconvenient but profound acts of kindness. Consider these few:

- Ruth showed kindness to Naomi by accompanying her to Bethlehem (Ruth 1).

- Jonathan showed kindness to David when Saul angrily hunted him (1 Samuel 18–20).

- David showed kindness to Mephibosheth by restoring his family's land (2 Samuel 9).

- The Shunammite woman showed kindness toward Elisha by preparing a room for him (2 Kings 4).

Many more examples could be given, but these demon-strate that kindness is a virtue that needs to be emulated by God's people. In the New Testament book of Ephesians, the apostle Paul helps to define and illustrate what it means to be kind.

 Read Ephesians 4:32.

What terms did Paul use in this verse to help describe what it means to "be kind to one another"?

_____

_____

_____

_____

_____

_____

_____

In your own words, how has God forgiven us in Christ? (If you're not quite sure how to answer this question, take a few minutes to read through the "How to Begin a Relationship with God" section on Page 87.)

_____

_____

_____

_____

_____

_____

_____

_____

_____

Do we need to do anything to gain God's kindness, favor, or forgiveness? Why, or why not? (See Ephesians 2:8–9.)

_____

_____

_____

_____

_____

_____

_____

_____

In what manner, then, are we expected to forgive others?

_____

_____

_____

_____

_____

_____

_____

_____

In light of these thoughts on forgiveness, consider Philippians 2:5–11. How might Christ's example influence our perspective regarding forgiveness?

_____

_____

_____

_____

_____

_____

In many ways, we are most like Christ when we forgive, show kindness, and demonstrate mercy—these are some of the most significant acts of Christian witness. Indeed, the hardest heart can be melted with the softest words of kindness.

JOSEPH'S KINDNESS

Millennia ago, there lived a young man who was about seventeen years old, whose large family of brothers despised him because of his favor with the Lord and with their father. They turned on him, came just short of murdering him, eventually selling him into slavery and faking his death in front of their father. Hatred, cruelty, abuse, humiliation . . . the young son of Israel, Joseph, experienced all of these at the hands of his siblings, men who should have been looking out for him. And though they had deceived their father, the two witnesses to the brothers' cruelty knew the truth: Joseph and God.

In spite of his ill treatment, the exceptionally gifted Joseph matured both physically and spiritually after being taken as a slave to Egypt. Though he suffered, Joseph overcame years of temptations, false accusations, abuse, imprisonment, and abandonment, all as he advanced in power and prominence through the Egyptian ranks. In a chain of events only the sovereign God could orchestrate, this young man grew into a stable, wise, and responsible adult who ultimately became the prime minister of Egypt, second only to the Pharaoh himself.

At this point in the account, the brothers who had betrayed Joseph unexpectedly came back into his life. When a famine struck the land of Canaan, Joseph's father sent his sons to buy grain from the Egyptians (Genesis 42:1–5). Little did they know that the person in charge of distributing grain during the famine was the brother they had brutalized years earlier. The sons of Jacob could have been in extreme danger, because Joseph had the authority to easily end their lives. He had the power to exact revenge, making them pay for their despicable sin.

But when the moment came to reveal his true identity, Joseph did something that would confuse, shock, and perhaps even anger anybody who knew the whole story: *he forgave his brothers.*

In the following sections, note the specific acts of kindness, mercy, and forgiveness exercised by Joseph.

Scripture	Joseph's Kindness
Genesis 43:16–25	
Genesis 45:1–14	
Genesis 47:11–12	

Knowing that they deserved revenge and retaliation, how do you think Joseph's brothers felt about his acts of kindness? (See Genesis 45:3, 5.)

_____

_____

_____

_____

_____

_____

_____

_____

What reasons did Joseph give for his kind and merciful response? (See Genesis 45:5–9.)

_____

_____

_____

_____

_____

_____

_____

_____

_____

After revealing his identity to his brothers, Joseph lavished blessings upon them—blessings they did not deserve. To save them from the famine, Joseph moved them to the land of Goshen (Genesis 47:1). There his elderly father, Jacob, lived the remainder of his life, and at 147 years old, Jacob blessed his twelve sons (Genesis 48–49), then breathed his last (49:33).

 Read Genesis 50:15–18.

Why do you think Joseph's brothers expected Joseph to seek revenge after Jacob was gone?

_____

_____

_____

_____

_____

_____

_____

_____

_____

_____

_____

Why was Joseph's unmerited, unconditional mercy, for-giveness, and kindness so difficult for the brothers to accept, even after all those years in Egypt?

Joseph's brothers fully expected that the sword of vengeance would fall on them after their father died. Were their expectations unreasonable from a human perspective? Of course not! They deserved punishment! What better time to let judgment fall than after the death of the one man who could have stopped it.

Read Genesis 50:19–21.

What reason did Joseph give for extending further kindness to his brothers?

In your own words, summarize the promise Joseph made to his brothers and their families. If you were in their shoes, what emotions would you feel? How would you respond?

_____

_____

_____

_____

_____

_____

_____

_____

_____

_____

Joseph never demanded that his brothers first repent, plead, or beg for mercy before he extended his mercy and kindness to them. In fact, he granted kindness before they even knew who he was! He never asked them to repay him or to make restitution for their acts of cruelty toward him. Instead, he repaid their cruelty with an abundance of mercy! Joseph had the right to demand justice, and he had the power to exact punishment. But instead, he granted mercy and exercised kindness. In his actions, Joseph typified the character of Christ, who granted mercy to us by paying the ultimate price, even while we were still sinners (Romans 5:8).

Digging Deeper
Love and Bitterness

Releasing bitterness is actually an act of unconditional love, as defined by Paul in 1 Corinthians 13:5—"[Love] does not take into account a wrong suffered." Love "keeps no record of wrongs" (1 Corinthians 13:5 NIV). Many of us fail to realize that holding a grudge not only destroys our relationship with the other person . . . it also destroys the one with the grudge.

In his book *What's So Amazing About Grace?* Philip Yancey writes:

> Not to forgive imprisons me in the past and locks out all potential for change. I thus yield control to another, my enemy, and doom myself to suffer the consequences of the wrong. I once heard an immigrant rabbi make an astonishing statement. "Before coming to America, I had to forgive Adolf

Hitler," he said. "I did not want to bring Hitler inside me to my new country."[3]

Even when we're genuinely wronged, Spirit-empowered love allows us to either overlook the offense or to forgive the offender and move on. Love doesn't dwell on the wrong or set invisible traps for the other person. Bitterness is actually a trap we set for ourselves, because failing to forgive ensnares us, wreaking havoc from the inside out.

This inconceivable, radical release of blame is perhaps best illustrated by the words of Christ on the cross. As observers blasphemed and ridiculed Him, He said, "Father, forgive them; for they do not know what they are doing" (Luke 23:34). If the Son of God, Creator and Ruler of the universe, can forgive His attackers, we can forgive those who have hurt us.

Joseph's painful life of hardship and suffering left him with a profound sense of God's providential care. All thoughts of revenge were removed. Every trace of bitterness had dissipated. His life was a model of kindness and Christlike love.

STARTING YOUR JOURNEY

We learn much from Joseph about the demonstration of kindness. Let's remember three principles as we examine our own attitudes and actions as they relate to Christlike kindness, mercy, and forgiveness.

First, *when we realize we're not in God's place, the desire for revenge fades away.* When Joseph's brothers expected his wrath after Jacob's death, Joseph said, "Do not be afraid, for am I in God's place?" (Genesis 50:19). His understanding that God was able to work through, with, and even in spite of his brothers' sin helped Joseph to trust in God's goodness even in the midst of people's wickedness.

Second, *when we acknowledge God's sovereign hand in all that happens, the grip of bitterness is loosened.* Joseph didn't deny that his brothers had done wrong. Nor did he forget. In fact, their evil deeds were eternally preserved in God's inspired Word, to be remembered for generations! But Joseph acknowledged that their evil was a part of God's good and perfect story—God permitted it, planning for His glory and Joseph's good . . . as well as for the good of Joseph's family. Our release of bitterness not only will mean forgiveness for others; it also will mean freedom for us.

Third, *when we are truly free of bitterness and revenge, there is plenty of room in our hearts for kindness.* Joseph exemplifies this by his kind actions—and his brothers were astounded by his willingness to forgive their evils. Forgiveness will not always be an easy road, but making the personal decision to replace bitterness and revenge with kindness and mercy is possible through the power of the Spirit.

As you reflect on your past or present relationships, can you think of someone who does not deserve your mercy, does not merit your forgiveness, and could never repay your kindness? Who is it? Describe your relationship with that person.

Read Romans 12:17–21. What thoughts, attitudes, people, or circumstances are keeping you from applying Paul's admonitions in these verses to the relationship you identified in the previous question?

_____

_____

_____

_____

_____

_____

_____

Sometimes healing from the harm people have inflicted on us requires much more than a simple decision to release bitterness. You may need pastors, wise, mature believers, or professional Christian counselors to help you work through relationships that have caused you pain. If the idea of showing kindness toward those who have harmed you seems unthinkable, who can you contact about helping you work through these issues in greater depth? Contact that person this week.

_____

_____

_____

_____

_____

_____

_____

_____

_____

If you have made the decision to release bitterness, to
forego revenge, and to embrace kindness and mercy, you
are ready to restore your broken relationship. How can
you express your kindness to this person through your
words or actions? Come up with at least three specific
ideas, then commit to acting on them this week.

_____

_____

_____

_____

_____

_____

_____

_____

_____

_____

Joseph's relationship with his brothers demonstrates incredible kindness. He not only overcame bitterness and the desire for revenge . . . he also demonstrated Christlike compassion that has become a model for our own attitudes and actions. If you've examined your life and found dark reserves of bitterness, make the decision to begin the process of releasing it today. God expects us to love kindness, to embrace mercy, and to forgive others, just as God in Christ has forgiven us (Ephesians 4:32).

Lesson Three

Modeling What's Humble

MICAH 6:8; 2 SAMUEL 16:5–13; PSALM 51:17

THE HEART OF THE MATTER

A silent battle rages in every one of us: the conflict between the sin of pride and the virtue of humility; the desire for significance versus the goal of becoming like Christ. We should not be surprised that when God told us what He expects of us through the prophet Micah, He included "Walk humbly with your God" (Micah 6:8). In the Old Testament, King David exemplifies humility for us in some surprising and helpful ways.

DISCOVERING THE WAY

Silently, behind the scenes of our public lives, the force of pride wages war against the virtue of humility. This ancient battle has claimed more victims than any disease, war, or disaster. But in the midst of the relentless lust for significance, power, and prestige that surrounds us, a lone voice calls to our hearts: "Take My yoke upon you and learn from Me, for I am gentle and humble in heart, and you will find rest for your souls" (Matthew 11:29). An invitation, a description, and a promise—the words sound so simple and easy to understand. But when we try to follow the path of Christ's humility, we quickly run into the barbed-wire battlement of pride. One Bible teacher vividly describes the manifestation of pride in our lives in this way:

Pride is a terrible trait, manifesting itself in our passion for the "best seats"—insisting on recognition, wanting to be noticed, longing for prominence, smarting when we're not consulted or advised, dominating social situations. It displays itself when we resist authority or become angry and defensive when crossed or challenged; when we harbor grudges, nurse grievances, or wallow in self-pity. It's the drive behind our penchant for associating with the rich and famous rather than the little people who make up most of our world.[1]

As you examine this description of pride, circle any traits that especially relate to your own life. Can you describe a recent experience from your life that would illustrate some of the traits you circled?

We all struggle with the sin of pride. Has it caused you to stumble or fall? How has it negatively affected your relationships?

_____

_____

_____

_____

_____

_____

Given pride's power to destroy our lives and the lives of those around us, it is no wonder that Micah highlighted humility as one of three things the Lord expects of us.

GOD EXPECTS US TO WALK HUMBLY

Micah told the people of Israel three things that the Lord expected from them: "to do justice, to love kindness, and to walk humbly with your God" (Micah 6:8). The Hebrew word translated as "walk humbly" is the word *tsana*, which normally means to "be modest, humble." But in this linguistic form, and within the context of Micah 6:8, it carries the meaning, "making humble to walk" with God.[2] It describes an outward action that flows from an inward attitude.

God's desire for His people to walk humbly with Him is not complicated or confusing, though actually putting His plan into practice can be extremely difficult for us, due to our sinful pride and our desire for significance and glory. So what does "walking humbly" actually look like in real life?

Read Philippians 2:3–4. What did Paul tell us to avoid in our relationships with others?

_____

_____

_____

_____

_____

_____

In your own words, what are we to do "with humility of mind" (Philippians 2:3)?

_____

_____

_____

_____

_____

_____

How should this inner attitude manifest itself outwardly in our actions (Philippians 2:4)? Be practical.

_____

_____

_____

_____

_____

_____

_____

According to Philippians 2:5, who is the ultimate model of humility?

_____

_____

_____

_____

_____

_____

   Walking humbly with God means being others-oriented. Humility includes a willingness to adjust our schedules and adapt our lives to the needs of others. The proud and self-serving have no room for that sort of thinking. But when we get stuck in our ways, spinning our wheels in the rut of pride, sin, and self-righteousness, God will step in. Sadly, humility does not come naturally for fallen people. To fashion this godly, Christlike humility, God must break the stubborn, selfish pride that hardens each of our hearts.

Digging Deeper
True Humility, True Exaltation

When it comes to our own ministry or career paths, we usually plan for a steady climb up the ladder of success or a periodic advancement to a better position. Rarely do we anticipate a step downward in pay, responsibility, or recognition. So when that happens, we may feel like failures or believe we're victims of injustice.

But if we recall Christ's path to exaltation in Philippians 2:6–11, we realize that the wisdom of this world regarding ambition is backwards. The path to true exaltation is humility . . . and the timing of our exaltation is in God's hands, not ours (1 Peter 5:6).

For Jesus, greatness came through humility, putting others above Himself, serving, and giving everything He had. We are responsible to follow Christ's example and to live humble lives, focusing on others and offering selfless acts of service. Getting to this level of humility takes confidence in our God and contentment with our circumstances, trusting that God will exalt us when and how He chooses, according to His goodness and sovereignty. Exaltation itself is not our responsibility, but God's prerogative (James 4:10).

DAVID'S HUMILITY

King David provides an example of a man who modeled humility through the crucible of crushing circumstances. If we were to sketch the pattern of humility and pride in his life, it would be shaped like this: ^. God raised him up from the valley of extreme humility to the mountaintop of extreme privilege. While still only a teenage shepherd, he was anointed king. He killed the giant Goliath when nobody else could. He became the personal musician of the King of Israel. And when he finally took the throne as King of Israel, he conquered his enemies, brought prosperity, expanded the borders of the land, and wrote inspired psalms of prophecy and praise.

But while he was at the peak of his success, pride set in. And his self-centered pride quickly turned into self-serving sin. The infamous account of David's adulterous affair with his neighbor Bathsheba (2 Samuel 11:1–4) should stir in us feelings of both disappointment and fear. But let's focus on what came *after* David's sin with Bathsheba, including his blundering attempts at covering it up and his murderous plot to avoid exposure (2 Samuel 11:5–27). David's power, position, and pride had converged, hardening his heart to his sin . . . and his heart could only be broken by God's intervention.

What events motivated David to cover up his sins? (See 2 Samuel 11:5–27.)

_____

_____

_____

_____

_____

_____

What emotions or fears might have also motivated David's cover-up? As you answer, try to place yourself in David's shoes.

_____

_____

_____

_____

_____

How do you think a humble spirit would have changed his attitudes and actions in this circumstance?

_____

_____

_____

_____

_____

_____

_____

_____

In response to his ever-hardening heart, God suddenly confronted David through the prophet Nathan (2 Samuel 12:1–12). God's light of truth exposed the darkness of David's lies. Then His fragrant Spirit of grace blew across the sour stench of unrepented sin. And David recognized the depth of his offense (2 Samuel 12:13).

After his humiliating encounter with Nathan, David retreated to a quiet place, poured out his tears before the Lord, and wrote the words of Psalm 51. Humility before God conquered David's fortress of pride.

Read Psalm 51:1–19.

Making no excuses, David focused on his own guilt and depravity before a just and holy God (Psalm 51:1–4).

He knew that cleansing, forgiveness, and restoration could come only by God's grace, not by any sacrifices or works he could offer (51:5–15). Broken and defeated, David humbly cast himself before God.

As you compare the following passages of Scripture, note the characteristics God does not want versus His expectations for a person with a humble heart.

	Micah 6:6–8	Psalm 51:16–17
God Does Not Want . . .		
God Wants . . .		

God forgave David, wiping his slate clean by His abundant mercy and grace. However, David still suffered earthly consequences as a result of his sin (2 Samuel 12:10–14). Following the sin with Bathsheba, David's life could be represented by the down-stroke of the ^. But, with a humble heart, David endured the trials and hardships.

When a person practices genuine humility, he or she places no blame on others, carries no grudges, and expects no rights or special treatment. A broken and contrite heart accepts the full weight of responsibility and considers all circumstances as being from the Lord. One brief episode from David's later life illustrates the attitude of humility wrought in his heart as the result of his brokenness.

As this episode opens, David's son Absalom had stolen the hearts of the people and usurped the throne of his father. Nathan's prophecy had come to pass (2 Samuel 12:11–12). Faced with his son's ultimate rebellion, David had a choice: to fight or to flee. He chose the latter. So, barefoot, broken-hearted, and beaten down, David and six hundred of his loyal followers fled Jerusalem and came to the village of Bahurim.

In this humble setting, David came face to face with public humiliation through an angry Israelite named Shimei.

Read 2 Samuel 16:5–8.

There's always one or two folks out there like Shimei, ready to hit us when we're down. They don't have all the facts. They lack wisdom, kindness, self-control, and grace. And they refuse to listen to reason. They take great pleasure in making their victims squirm. When faced with such people, we have two options: we can attack them or we can take their insults.

What do you think David's natural response would be to the ravings of a man like Shimei?

_____

_____

_____

_____

_____

_____

_____

_____

How would David be justified in responding this way?

_____

_____

_____

_____

_____

_____

_____

_____

Read 2 Samuel 16:9–13.

In response to Shimei's attacks, David humbled himself before God. He didn't confront the assaults with a counterattack. Nor did he agree with everything that came from his critic's lips. And he didn't silently seethe and fume. Rather, he responded in two ways that serve as a model of patient humility for us:

First, *David considered God's hand in the criticism* (2 Samuel 16:10–11). David fully acknowledged his plight. Instead of simply saying "Consider the source" and dismissing him as a lunatic, David's strategy exhibited real humility: "Consider the criticism." In meekness and humility, we can learn a lesson even from harsh, heartless criticism when we are willing to recognize God's plan in all things.

Second, *David refused to defend himself* (2 Samuel 16:12–13). Not once did David call attention to himself, naming all his heroic deeds from the past. He could have summoned a résumé a mile long to outweigh Shimei's short list of criticisms, but instead David opted for humility. Rather than vindicating himself, he placed his trust in God.

Put yourself in the shoes of those who were following and supporting David. What do you think they may have thought about David's response? Do you think their respect for him increased or decreased? Why?

_____

_____

_____

_____

_____

_____

_____

_____

_____

_____

David turned the attack on his character and his wounded pride over to His sovereign God: "If he curses, and if the LORD has told him, 'Curse David,' then who shall say, 'Why have you done so? . . . Perhaps the LORD will look on my affliction and return good to me instead of his cursing this day'" (2 Samuel 16:10, 12). David knew that vengeance belonged to the Lord and that he was weak and needy (see Psalm 109:21–31). St. Augustine reflected this sentiment well when he asked to be delivered from the "lust of vindicating myself."[3] In many cases, self-vindication is the opposite of walking humbly before God.

STARTING YOUR JOURNEY

God's desire for us to walk humbly leads to three practical benedictions.

First, *may we see pride as our archenemy and refuse its lure.* Reject pride's demand for self-vindication. Pride often brings with it the defense of rationalization, the temptation of self-ishness, and the allure of plain common sense. It appeals to your sense of entitlement, of rights, of getting what you know you deserve. It even appeals to Scripture on occasion (and often out of context). But all self-serving pride is our enemy.

According to Proverbs 27:2, where should your praise come from?

_____

_____

_____

_____

_____

_____

_____

_____

_____

_____

_____

_____

How have you been engaging in self-promotion lately? Be honest.

_____

_____

_____

_____

_____

_____

_____

_____

_____

Second, *may we embrace humility as our friend and let things be.* Taking on the world's problems as your own will not usher in God's kingdom. Pride not only whispers that it's all about you, but that you're the only one who can get things done right. As a fallen, finite people living under the sovereign hand of an infinite God, we need to embrace humility and trust God's perfect plan.

Has this lesson helped you to recognize an area of ambition or pursuit, fueled by pride, that you need to release to God? Note it here, and ask God to take it from you.

_____

_____

_____

_____

_____

_____

_____

_____

_____

_____

_____

_____

Third, *may we return to the cross where Christ nailed the sin of pride and modeled humility.* Proud men crucified the Lord—protecting their power, vindicating their authority, asserting their rights and privileges. Many were fueled by envy and avarice, but many others thought they were taking God's work into their own hands. Don't follow their example of pride. Rather, pursue Christ's example of a gentle, humble spirit. Don't ever forget who won the ultimate battle through silence and patient endurance.

Over the next week or so, take time to memorize Philippians 2:3–9. Meditate not only on Paul's exhortation to humility, but also on the profound example of Christ's humiliation. Begin now by writing out the verses in the following space.

This lesson helped us to surface subtle areas of pride in our lives—circumstances in which we may feel justified to defend ourselves or to attack our attackers. But we are better off walking humbly before God and allowing Him to work on our behalf. David's example of humility and Christ's emptying of Himself for our sakes should encourage us to lay down our rights and embrace the virtue of humility. Will you make a commitment today to "walk humbly with your God"?

Lesson Four

Enjoying the Rewards

DANIEL 6:1–4

THE HEART OF THE MATTER

We all need heroes to inspire and challenge us to live authentic lives of integrity. Centuries ago, one such hero, a man of faultless integrity, kept afloat in the swamps of ethical compromise. His name was Daniel, and he serves as an example of authenticity for us as we seek to become people of integrity in our own generation. A life well lived not only inspires others, but also results in great reward both in this world and in the world to come.

DISCOVERING THE WAY

Superheroes seem more popular today than ever. Television programs, blockbuster films, toys, and books showcase an array of crime-fighting characters that the previous generation could find only in the pages of a comic book.

This increased interest in superhero sagas begs the question—what makes a real hero? Attaining the status of a hero used to require that a person be an exceptional role model and accomplish amazing feats of physical strength, intellectual prowess, or uncommon courage. But today's hero accomplishes a unique set of otherworldly exploits: doing what's right, loving mercy, and walking humbly before God. Such a person, armed with authenticity and integrity, stands out from the crowd.

However, the public images of many of our heroes, like presidents, teachers, and pastors, have been maimed by scandal and hypocrisy over the last couple of generations. We're living at a time when those who do what's right, love kindness, and model humility occupy thin ranks.

The time has come to repopulate those ranks with men and women of authenticity . . . godly leaders with integrity . . . with a new generation of heroes.

The dictionary defines *integrity* as "an unimpaired condition or "the quality or state of being complete or undivided."[1] How would you define integrity?

_____

_____

_____

_____

_____

_____

Name some inanimate objects or ideas that have integrity, according to your definition. Or draw a picture of something that has integrity.

_____

_____

_____

_____

_____

_____

_____

_____

Think of several people whom you consider to have integrity. What qualities do you see in them that demonstrate integrity?

_____

_____

_____

_____

_____

_____

_____

_____

THE NEED FOR INTEGRITY

Now that we've carefully defined the concept of integrity, let's consider one of its most important components: authenticity. The word *authenticity* implies genuineness—outward actions and words that accurately reflect the inward attitudes of the heart and mind. Only authentic people—those who live their lives without hypocrisy—can be people of integrity.

Read the following proverbs, and note at least one truth in each one that describes why integrity is necessary in our lives.

According to This Proverb . . .	Integrity Is Needed Because . . .
Proverbs 10:9	
Proverbs 11:3	
Proverbs 20:6–7	
Proverbs 28:1	
Proverbs 29:10	

Which of the needs described in the chart resonate most with your current circumstances? Why did you choose this particular one?

_____

_____

_____

_____

_____

_____

_____

_____

_____

We live in an age when people of integrity and authenticity are in short supply. So widespread are the problems of duplicity, deception, and hypocrisy in our world that these have penetrated the ranks of Christian leaders and lay people alike. Sadly, research confirms this troubling notion. After studying the ethical standards of those who claim to be Christians, Doug Sherman and William Hendricks concluded that the ethical conduct of Christians is only slightly better than that of non-Christians. From healthy employees calling in sick to otherwise honest folks fudging on their income tax forms, Christians commit the same kinds of sins as non-Christians—and almost to the same degree.[2]

Answer the following questions honestly:

Have You Ever . . .		
Given inaccurate or incomplete information on a form?	Yes	No
Told a "harmless" lie to your spouse?	Yes	No
Shifted blame to somebody else to keep from getting into trouble?	Yes	No
Conducted personal business or goofed off during work hours?	Yes	No
Consciously and intentionally exceeded the speed limit?	Yes	No
Copied software, music, or a video that you did not own?	Yes	No

If you answered "Yes" to any of these questions, you can join the millions of other Christians who struggle daily with living an authentic life in the midst of a corrupt and perverse world. In short, we all could use a daily boost of integrity.

Digging Deeper
Integrity and the Cause of Christ
Jesus said, "Let your light shine before men in such a way that they may see your good works, and glorify your Father who is in heaven" (Matthew 5:16). And Peter wrote, "Keep your behavior excellent

among the Gentiles, so that in the thing in which they slander you as evildoers, they may because of your good deeds, as they observe them, glorify God in the day of visitation" (1 Peter 2:12).

How tragic that so many Christians today are often clothed in scandal, exposed as frauds, or revealed as self-serving hypocrites. If our good works were meant to woo people to God and the gospel, what damages have our bad works inflicted upon the cause of Christ?

One Christian writer notes:

> As I travel extensively and read widely and hear frequently from friends in a variety of work settings, I cannot agree that Christians—"true" Christians—in our society are better behaved ethically at work than their non-Christian coworkers. They—that is, *we*—ought to be. We have the spiritual resources to be. But the sad reality is, with few exceptions, we aren't.[3]

Without authenticity and integrity permeating every aspect of our lives, we run the risk of losing

> our family, ministry, job, and reputation. But the reality is much worse than that. Not only do we risk ourselves and those close to us, we run the serious risk of marring the reputation of God's people and, by extension, God Himself.

DANIEL, A MAN YOU COULD TRUST

Given the statistical reality of Christian dishonesty, an examination of our own hearts, and the proof from countless examples of moral failure in Scripture, it would be easy to believe that we can't trust anyone. And what's worse, we might begin to believe that a life of integrity will only be available to us when Christ returns.

Quickly put away such fatalistic words of surrender. Though the righteous remnant has always been a minority, men and women of integrity continue to provide enough light along life's path to give us hope. As we look into the pages of Scripture, one of these lights shines brightly among the others: the Old Testament prophet Daniel.

A victim of the Babylonian captivity of Israel six centuries before Christ's birth, Daniel found himself and his Hebrew friends exiled in a foreign land of idolatry, wickedness, and corruption. And with cultural floodwaters rushing toward a moral and religious abyss, Daniel stood his ground. He demonstrated the integrity of his heart to both friend and foe—and God rewarded him for his life well lived.

Read Daniel 6:1–4.

How remarkable that Daniel—a foreigner from a vanquished nation—ascended the ranks of the pagan kingdom of Darius the Mede! So highly did God exalt him that he was one of only three commissioners supervising 120 administrators of the king. Today, if we were to witness such a skyrocketing career, we would probably be right to suppose that such a person achieved his or her success through underhanded means. In fact, those in Daniel's day suspected as much (Daniel 6:4)! But in Daniel's case, their assumption was completely wrong.

Why do you think the commissioners and satraps wanted to dig up some dirt on Daniel? What was their primary motivation?

_____

_____

_____

_____

_____

_____

What do you think motivates people today to point out hypocrisy among believers?

_____

_____

_____

_____

_____

_____

_____

If a team of investigative reporters decided to target you, seeking to find grounds for accusation, evidence of corruption, or proof of negligence, would you be afraid of what they might uncover? Why, or why not?

_____

_____

_____

_____

_____

_____

_____

By this point, almost every person reading this lesson will likely have identified some nagging area that suffers from an integrity deficit. You may have surfaced several. In the space on the left of the following chart, write the one area of your life that needs the most work in order to increase your integrity. Jot down some of the negative qualities you see in yourself that accompany this integrity lapse. In the column on the far right, describe positive character qualities you would like to see replace the negatives. Your goal should be the complete opposite of your need.

After examining your present condition and comparing it to your desired goal, take some time through prayer, reflection, and even discussions with others to come up with about six steps you can take to move closer to your goal of authenticity and integrity. Make your steps concrete and measurable, such as "Read a book about honesty in marriage by the end of the month" or "Meet with the pastor this week to discuss my addiction." (At the end of the chapter, you will return to complete the remainder of this chart.)

Need   **Goal**

Steps

Qualities: 1._____   **Qualities:**

_____   2._____   _____

_____   3._____   _____

_____   4._____   _____

_____   5._____   _____

_____   6._____   _____

Proposing a plan for boosting integrity is only half the assignment. Now, select one of these steps and actually do it, regardless of how difficult or time-consuming it might be.

 STARTING YOUR JOURNEY
Rare though they may be, a few real heroes still sojourn in this fallen world—men and women like Daniel who confront corruption and survive temptation, who epitomize a life well lived with justice, mercy, humility, and integrity. For such rare diamonds, who are often lost among a field of broken glass, the Lord God has promised great rewards. These rewards are not only for the "super saints," but for all of us who, by faith, desire to live our lives God's way.

First, *a life well lived cultivates exemplary character.* Character transformation never comes instantly. Hebrews 5:14 tells us that maturity comes as the result of "practice," which, over the course of time, trains the senses to discern good and evil. And Peter implied a similar process of development and growth when he delineated the qualities that characterize a fruitful Christian life (2 Peter 1:5–8). Constant attention to unseen character traits will result in a godly reputation among both believers and unbelievers.

Second, *a life well lived is accompanied by the continued relief of a clear conscience.* You know the feeling—wringing your hands, hoping that nobody finds out what you did . . . tossing and turning with red-eyed insomnia as you play a regretted action over and over in your mind . . . avoiding eye contact with certain people because you're afraid they'll see through your deception. But when you do what is right, show kindness, and walk humbly, all with integrity, your conscience will be free from the aches and pains that accompany corrupt living.

Third, *a life well lived leads to the personal delight of intimacy with the Almighty.* While sin disrupts our personal relationship with God, doing what God expects of us brings us closer to Him. An intimate relationship with the Almighty will spill over into other relationships as well, as you share the grace and love you experience with others, also inviting them into a relationship with God.

Fourth, *a life well lived invests in the priceless inheritance of a lingering legacy.* Just as the heroes and heroines of yesteryear continue to shine, guiding our paths today, so will the legacy of your life outlive your mortal body. The people you will impact, the example you will set, the lessons you will teach—these things will echo into the future and continue to reverberate in the lives of people you have never even met.

Fifth, *a life well lived can provide the rare privilege of being a mentor.* One of the most wonderful privileges afforded to a woman or man of integrity who leads a life worth emulating is the opportunity to mentor someone else. More than a teacher, leader, or companion, a mentor provides close, hands-on guidance to those who need an example to follow. When you live a life pleasing to God, people will seek you out and ask to be discipled by you. There is no greater privilege in the world.

Sixth, *a life well lived results in the crowning reward of finishing well*. Those who diligently pursue the path of justice, mercy, humility, and integrity are guaranteed to finish well. But if we become distracted from the road by temptations, bitterness, pride, or corruption, we will become a shameful example to be avoided rather than a brilliant hero long remembered.

Of the above rewards, which one seems to motivate you the most to pursue the path of a life well lived?

_____

_____

_____

_____

_____

_____

_____

_____

Why do you think this particular benefit speaks to you more than the others?

_____

_____

_____

_____

_____

_____

_____

Return to the need and goal chart on page 81. Write your chosen benefit of a life well lived on the line below the chart as a motivating reward for accomplishing the steps before you.

Rest assured that the rewards of a life well lived far exceed anything you can hope to achieve by compromising the truth, harboring bitterness, pursuing pride, or living a double life. God's way of life is simple, and most important of all, He dwells inside you by His Spirit to give you the ability to accomplish His will. This world, filled with so many tragic examples of failure and rebellion, calls out for more heroes.

Will you answer that call by living your life well?

*How to Begin
a Relationship
with God*

Micah 6:8 tells us what the Lord expects of His people: to do justice, to love kindness, and to walk humbly before God. Some may believe that this is a formula for beginning a relationship with God. But the reality is quite different. Micah's prescription for a well-lived life actually presupposes a relationship with God. Before we can seek to live this kind of life, we must receive new life itself. So, what does the Lord require of a person who wants to begin a relationship with Him?

Let's take a look at what Scripture says about this life-giving relationship. The Bible marks the path to God with four essential truths. We'll look at each marker in detail.

Our Spiritual Condition: Totally Depraved

The first truth is rather personal. One look in the mirror of Scripture, and our human condition becomes painfully clear:

> There is none righteous, not even one;
> There is none who understands,
> There is none who seeks for God;
> All have turned aside, together they have
>   become useless;
> There is none who does good,
> There is not even one. (Romans 3:10–12)

We are all sinners through and through—totally depraved. Now, that doesn't mean we've committed every atrocity known to humankind. We're not as *bad* as we can be, just as *bad off* as we can be. Sin colors all our thoughts, motives, words, and actions.

You still don't believe it? Look around. Everything around us bears the smudge marks of our sinful nature. Despite our best efforts to create a perfect world, crime statistics continue to soar, divorce rates keep climbing, and families keep crumbling.

Something has gone terribly wrong in our society and in ourselves—something deadly. Contrary to how the world would repackage it, "me-first" living doesn't equal rugged individuality and freedom; it equals death. As Paul said in his letter to the Romans, "The wages of sin is death" (Romans 6:23)—our spiritual and physical death that comes from God's righteous judgment of our sin, along with all of the emotional and practical effects of this separation that we experience on a daily basis. This brings us to the second marker: God's character.

GOD'S CHARACTER: INFINITELY HOLY

How can a good and just God judge us for a sinful state into which we were born? Our total depravity is only half the answer. The other half is God's infinite holiness.

The fact that we know things are not as they should be points us to a standard of goodness beyond ourselves. Our sense of injustice in life on this side of eternity implies a perfect standard of justice beyond our reality. That standard and source is God Himself. And God's standard of holiness contrasts starkly with our sinful condition.

Scripture says that "God is Light, and in Him there is no darkness at all" (1 John 1:5). He is absolutely holy—which creates a problem for us. If He is so pure, how can we who are so impure relate to Him?

Perhaps we could try being better people, try to tilt the balance in favor of our good deeds, or seek out methods for self-improvement. Throughout history, people have attempted to live up to God's standard by keeping the Ten Commandments or living by their own code of ethics. Unfortunately, no one can come close to satisfying the demands of God's law. Romans 3:20 says, "For no one can ever be made right with God by doing what the law commands. The law simply shows us how sinful we are" (NLT).

OUR NEED: A SUBSTITUTE

So here we are, sinners by nature and sinners by choice, trying to pull ourselves up by our own bootstraps to attain a relationship with our holy Creator. But every time we try, we fall flat on our faces. We can't live a good enough life to make up for our sin, because God's standard isn't "good enough"—it's *perfection*. And we can't make amends for the offense our sin has created without dying for it.

Who can get us out of this mess?

If someone could live perfectly, honoring God's law, and would bear sin's death penalty for us—in our place— then we would be saved from our predicament. But is there such a person? Thankfully, yes!

Meet your substitute—*Jesus Christ*. He is the One who took death's place for you!

> [God] made [Jesus Christ] who knew no sin to
> be sin on our behalf, so that we might become
> the righteousness of God in Him.
> (2 Corinthians 5:21)

GOD'S PROVISION: A SAVIOR

God rescued us by sending His Son, Jesus, to die for our sins on the cross (1 John 4:9–10). Jesus was fully human and fully divine (John 1:1, 18), a truth that ensures His understanding of our weaknesses, His power to forgive, and His ability to bridge the gap between God and us (Romans 5:6–11). In short, we are "justified as a gift by His grace through the redemption which is in Christ Jesus" (Romans 3:24). Two words in this verse bear further explanation: *justified* and *redemption*.

Justification is God's act of mercy, in which He declares believing sinners righteous while they are still in their sinning state. Justification doesn't mean that God *makes* us righteous, so that we never sin again, rather that He *declares* us righteous—much like a judge pardons a guilty criminal. Because Jesus took our sin upon Himself and suffered our judgment on the cross, God forgives our debt and proclaims us PARDONED.

Redemption is God's act of paying the ransom price to release us from our bondage to sin. Held hostage by Satan, we were shackled by the iron chains of sin and death. Like a loving parent whose child has been kidnapped, God willingly paid the ransom for you. And what a price He paid! He gave His only Son to bear our sins—past, present, and future. Jesus's death and resurrection broke our chains and set us free to become children of God (Romans 6:16–18, 22; Galatians 4:4–7).

PLACING YOUR FAITH IN CHRIST

These four truths describe how God has provided a way to Himself through Jesus Christ. Because the price has been paid in full by God, we must respond to His free gift of eternal life in total faith and confidence in Him to save us. We must step forward into the relationship with God that He has prepared for us—not by doing good works or by being good people, but by coming to Him just as we are and accepting His justification and redemption by faith.

> For by grace you have been saved through faith; and that not of yourselves, it is the gift of God; not as a result of works, so that no one may boast. (Ephesians 2:8–9)

We accept God's gift of salvation simply by placing our faith in Christ alone for the forgiveness of our sins. Would you like to enter a relationship with your Creator by trusting in Christ as your Savior? If so, here's a simple prayer you can use to express your faith:

Dear God,

I know that my sin has put a barrier between You and me. Thank You for sending Your Son, Jesus, to die in my place. I trust in Jesus alone to forgive my sins, and I accept His gift of eternal life. I ask Jesus to be my personal Savior and the Lord of my life. Thank You.

In Jesus's name, Amen.

If you've prayed this prayer or one like it and you wish to find out more about knowing God and His plan for you in the Bible, contact us at Insight for Living.

Pastoral Ministries Department
Insight for Living
Post Office Box 269000
Plano, Texas USA 75026-9000
972-473-5097
(Monday through Friday,
8:00 AM—5:00 PM Central time)
www.insight.org/contactapastor

Endnotes

Lesson 1

Unless otherwise noted below, all material in this chapter is adapted from "Doing What's Right," a sermon by Charles R. Swindoll, and supplemented by the Creative Ministries department of Insight for Living.

1. R. Laird Harris, Gleason L. Archer, and Bruce K. Waltke, *Theological Wordbook of the Old Testament*, vol. 2 (Chicago: Moody Press, 1980), 949.

2. Martin Luther, *Werke*, Erl. Frkf. ed., vol. LXIV, 382, as quoted in Philip Schaff, *History of the Christian Church*, vol. VII, *Modern Christianity: The German Reformation* (Grand Rapids: Eerdmans, 1950), 305n1. Translation by Michael J. Svigel.

Lesson 2

Unless otherwise noted below, all material in this chapter is adapted from "Loving What's Kind," a sermon by Charles R. Swindoll, and supplemented by the Creative Ministries department of Insight for Living.

1. Bob Hercules and Cheri Pugh, directors, *Forgiving Dr. Mengele*, documentary (2005).

2. Francis Brown, S. R. Driver, and Charles A. Briggs, eds., *The Brown-Driver-Briggs Hebrew and English Lexicon* (Peabody, Mass.: Hendrickson, 1996), 338–339.

3. Philip Yancey, *What's So Amazing About Grace?* (Grand Rapids: Zondervan, 1997), 99.

Lesson 3

Unless otherwise noted below, all material in this chapter is adapted from "Modeling What's Humble," a sermon by Charles R. Swindoll, and supplemented by the Creative Ministries department of Insight for Living.

1. *A Burden Shared*, Copyright © 1991 by David Roper. Used by permission of Discovery House Publishers, Grand Rapids, MI 49501. All rights reserved.

2. Francis Brown, S. R. Driver, and Charles A. Briggs, eds., *The Brown-Driver-Briggs Hebrew and English Lexicon* (Peabody, Mass.: Hendrickson, 1996), 857.

3. Augustine, *Confessions* 10.36.58. In Philip Schaff, ed., *Nicene and Post-nicene Fathers*, vol. 1, *The Confessions and Letters of Augustine, with a Sketch of His Life and Work*, A Select Library of the Christian Church, First Series (New York: Christian Literature, 1886; reprint, Peabody, Mass.: Hendrickson, 1994), 159.

Lesson 4

Unless otherwise noted below, all material in this chapter is adapted from "Enjoying the Rewards," a sermon by Charles R. Swindoll, and supplemented by the Creative Ministries department of Insight for Living.

1. *Merriam-Webster's Collegiate Dictionary*, 11th ed. (Springfield, Mass.: Merriam-Webster, 2003), see "integrity."

2. Doug Sherman and William Hendricks, *Keeping Your Ethical Edge Sharp* (Colorado Springs: NavPress, 1990), 29–30.

3. Doug Sherman and William Hendricks, *Keeping Your Ethical Edge Sharp*, 31.

Discover the reality of godly living in Charles Swindoll's latest book *A Life Well Lived.*

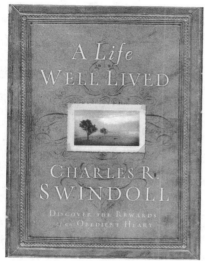

ISBN 978-0-8499-0189-8 • $14.99 U.S.

"Am I living a life that delights God?"
"What does He expect of me?"

Do you constantly wonder what it takes to live the way God intends? Be encouraged! God's Word provides a clear answer. In a crooked culture all too similar to our own, the Old Testament prophet Micah offered a divinely inspired prescription for living life well in the midst of a fallen, sin-twisted world. God's expectations for His children are simple and direct, and He promises to reward an obedient heart.

In *A Life Well Lived*, Chuck Swindoll digs deeply into these practical principles from God's Word and applies them to real life. As you read, you'll have the opportunity to examine your life in the light of God's desires for His people, discovering exactly what He expects of you as one of His own. And you'll be inspired to please God by living your life well!

THOMAS NELSON
Since 1798